# PERSIUS REDUX

# PERSIUS REDUX

A Translation of the Satires of Persius
(Aulus Persius Flaccus)

*Inspired by the Unlettered Muse*

Translated by Theodore B. Guérard

THE HIGHLAND LAKE PRESS, *Publishers*

With appreciation for the College of Charleston Department of Classics and their mission to promote an understanding of the ancient Greek and Roman world and its legacy through an investigation of the languages and cultures of these civilizations. All proceeds from the sale of this book benefit the Theodore Guérard Fund at the College.

ISBN 978-0-578-46892-1

# CONTENTS

# INTRODUCTION

*Aulus Persius Flaccus* was born December 4, A.D. 34, at Volaterræ, in Etruria (approximately the modern Tuscany) of a father of equestrian rank and modest wealth who died when Persius was six. At 12, he was sent to Rome to study under a noted grammarian and a noted rhetorician. When he was 16, he placed himself under the guidance of a famous Stoic philosopher, Annaeus Cornutus. Persius formed a lifetime relationship with this friend and teacher, and became a disciple of Stoicism.

It is reported that his reading of the tenth book of Lucilius so impressed him that he undertook the composition of satires. His poems were received with applause as soon as they appeared and received high praise from Quintilian and Martial. They were favorites of the Latin fathers, quoted or imitated by Augustine and Jerome. Persius died November 24, A.D. 62, in his twenty-eighth year, leaving six Satires, which form a *libellus* of 650 hexameters.

Although much read in antiquity and the Middle Ages, Persius is now little read. This Translation is an attempt to restore the popularity of Persius by eliminating the perceived obscurities I have found in the several translations with which I am familiar. For example, Satires IV and VI present difficulties of sense when read as single satires. But when these Satires are treated as medleys of several satires, loosely connected, if connected at all (in the form inherited by Persius from Lucilius), the obscurities disappear and we have interesting and lively vignettes of first-century Roman life, which would indicate that perceived obscurities may lie not in Persius' text, but rather in the translations.

I am not a Latin scholar in the usual sense of the term. My academic background consists of an A.B. Degree in English (with the required four years of Latin) from the College of Charleston, Charleston, S.C., in 1950, and courses taken there over the past six years in Latin poetry, one of which included Persius. Nevertheless I have undertaken this work, perhaps in response to the implied invitation in Professor Gildersleeve's observation "of the way in which the text of [Persius] has been smothered in learning." And it is in an effort to be candid that this Translation is subtitled "Inspired by the Unlettered Muse," a reference derived from Gray's *Elegy Written in a Country Churchyard:*

> *Their names, their years, spelt by the unlettered Muse,*
> *The place of fame and elegy supply;*
> *And many a holy text around she strews*
> *That teach the rustic moralist to die.*

THEODORE B. GUÉRARD, A.B., J.D.
*Charleston, S.C.*
*October 1996*

# Translation

*English*

# SATIRE I

## Summary of Satire I

Contemporary poetry that shuns political and social criticism and embraces sensual sound without regard for the quality of content is the subject of this satire. Persius deplores the public performance of such verse (lines 1-28); to the argument that poets naturally want to establish a reputation, he responds that a reputation for trash is worthless (lines 29-47); he agrees that worthwhile poetry is entitled to praise, but calls Rome's standard for acceptance a mockery (lines 47-64) and dishonest (lines 65-75).

Persius is indignant that the people are beguiled to be satisfied by mere words and smoothness of verse (lines 76-83) and that poetasters fond of Greek along with worthless and melodramatic poems of the past are corrupting the teaching of children and encouraging public displays of effeminacy (lines 84-100). He scorns the practice of the court with its emphasis on polished phrases intended to divert and mislead (lines 101-112); and ridicules the argument that worthwhile elegance and smoothness are brought to verse by contemporary poets (lines 113-130).

Finally, though warned he may suffer retaliation, Persius expresses his determination to pursue the writing of critical, honest satires and seeks readers who will be moved to anger by his verse (lines 131-163).

## Satire I Verse

*Of the things men concern themselves with; O, how much of these*
*matters is useless!* Who will read these? "Are you asking that
question of me?" No one, by Hercules! "Nobody?" One
or two. "A disgrace and pitiable." Wherefore? So that
Polydamus and the Trojan ladies will be putting                     5
Labeo above me? No matter. Do not come near the
faulty tongue on that scale of Rome's to correct whatever
muddled Rome belittles, nor seek beyond yourself. For at
Rome, who is not. . .? Ah, would that it were fair to say—but then
fair it is after I have looked at the gray heads and this          10
dreary life of ours and the things we do when our toys have
been laid aside and we taste responsibility. Then,
then, disregard me. "I won't do that." What am I to do?
But I am a scoffer with a saucy sense of humor.

We closet ourselves and write, that one poetry, this one          15
prose, something which we think is mighty, which a lung pants forth
with a lot of air. Yes, certainly, well combed, in a fresh
toga, wearing your birthday stone, dressed all in white and sitting
upon a lofty seat, at last you will read these to the
people, after you have washed your throat with a clear gargle          20
until it becomes compliant, distracted only by
your wanton glances. Now one would see the huge sons of Rome,
without self-control and with a discomposed sound, quiver
when the strains sink into the loins and the intimate
sensations respond to the tremulous verse. Old man, are          25
you composing stimulations for the ears of others
which, if they were offered to you, you would say that you are
too diseased to enjoy?

               "What is the purpose to have learned
unless this yeast and the wild fig with its fruit, once it          30
has been born within, bursts forth from an open heart?" Behold,
whence your pallor and signs of age! O, such foolishness! Is
what you know of no worth at all unless another knows
you know it? "But it is admirable to be pointed
at and 'This is he!' to be said. Would you count it nothing          35
to have been the text for one hundred curlyhead school boys?"

Behold the men of Rome, having overeaten and in
their cups, ask what do the divine poems tell. Hereupon
somebody, his gaily colored cloak around his shoulders,
speaking something loathsome from his snuffling nose, Phyllidas          40
Hypsipylas, and whatever of the brotherhood is
deplorable, filters his words and trips them off of his
palate. The gentlemen express their approval; now are
not those ashes of the poet fortunate? Now does not a
lighter stone press upon his bones? The guests applaud. Will not          45
now from those shades, will not now from the tomb and the lucky
ashes, violets spring forth? "You are making fun," he says,
"and indulging your nose in too much twitting. So then, will
there be anyone who denies the wish to have earned the

people's applause, and having spoken words worthy to be          50
preserved in cedar oil, to leave behind him songs fearful
of neither mackerels nor incense?"[1]

                    Whoever you are
whom I have fashioned to speak in disagreement, when I
write, if by some chance anything does come forth rather fine,          55
since this is a rare bird, nevertheless if anything
does come forth rather fine, I will not fear to be praised, and
truly my heart is not of horn; but I deny that your
"Well done" and "Elegantly" are the standard and last word
of correctness. For shake out all of this "Elegantly,"          60
what does it not hold within? Is not here Attius's
Iliad, drunk of hellebore? Is not here whatever cute
elegy the dyspeptic gentlemen have repeated?
In short, anything written on the couches of citron?
You know how to serve up a warm sow's udder, you know how          65
to give a rough-looking dependent a worn-out cloak; and
you say "I love truth; tell me the truth about myself." Who
can do that? Calvus,[2] would you want me to say, "You write trash,"
when, thanks to you, my stomach is growing plump by a good
foot and a half. O, fortunate Ianus,[3] behind whose back          70
no stork claps and no moving hands imitate the donkey's
white ears, nor is there so much of a tongue as a thirsty
Apulian dog shows. You, O noble blood, whose fate it
is to live with a blind back, turn around, meet the grimaces
behind.          75
                    And what is the conversation of the people?
"What, indeed, except that now at last the poetry flowed with

---

[1] *i.e.,* Not fearful of becoming wrapping for mackerel or incense.
[2] A reference to Gaius Licinius Calvus (82-?47 B.C.), orator and poet who practiced the style of the Athenians which Persius deplores. Cf. v. 84 et seq, *infra.*
[2] A reference to Gaius Licinius Calvus (82-?47 B.C.), orator and poet who practiced the style of the Athenians which Persius deplores. Cf. v. 84 et seq, *infra.*
[3] Roman god with a face in front and behind.

tender phrasing[4] and he has learned to lay out, as if he
were setting straight a red line with one eye, the verse he may
as a consequence pour forth past the rigid fingernails                    80
with a smooth juncture.[5] Whether the work speaks out about
morals, about debauchery, about banquets of the
rich, the Muse gives to our poet sublime resources!"

                                 Behold, now
we see those accustomed to talk nonsense in Greek bring forth              85
heroic sentiments who are not skillful to picture
scenery, nor to praise the plenteous countryside where
there are baskets and the hearth and pigs and the festival
of Pales reeking in smoke; whence comes Remus, and, wearing
away his plowshares in the furrow, thou Quinctius,[6] whom            90
your anxious wife before oxen clothed dictator and the
Lictor carried home your plow—Well, done, Poet!

                                There is one now
whom the wrinkled book of Bacchic Accius entrances
and there are whom Pacuvius and warty Antiope,                             95
her heart supported by grief bringing hardships, captivate.
When you see blear-eyed fathers provide these as instructions
for their children, do you ask whence this jumble of language
has come, whence this disgrace to which your effeminate sons
of Rome jump up and down along the benches on the floor?             100

Is there no shame in being unable to put on trial
an old gray beard but you must first listen for a lukewarm
compliment? "You are a thief," he says to Pedius. What
does Pedius do? He balances the charges upon
polished antitheses: to phrase clever figures of speech                   105
is praised. "This is lovely!" Is this lovely? Or, Romulus,

---

[4] Refers to language used; e.g., lines 40-43, *supra*, lines 120-25, *infra*.

[5] Referring to the smooth flow of the verse; e.g., lines 113-17; 120-25, *infra*. The confluence of successive syllables and words of the poet's verse is as smooth as the meeting of two pieces of marble whose flush faces are cut so straight that a rigid fingernail drawn across the juncture feels no seam. The straight line in this metaphor would run not parallel but perpendicular to the verse between successive words and syllables.

[6] Quinctius Cincinnatus.

are you squirming? Would it move me? Indeed, if a
shipwrecked sailor should sing, would I offer him a penny?

You are singing although you should be carrying yourself on
your shoulders painted on a ship's broken timber;[7] the truth,          110
and not something dreamed up. He must cry out in grief who wants
me to bend with his lament.

                          "But elegance and smoothness
have been brought to rough feet. He has learned to close a verse thus,
*Berecyntius Attis* and          115
*qui cœruleum diremebat Nerea delphin,* and so
*costem longo subduximus Appennine.*
Is not *Arma Virum*[8] full of foam and with a dense bark,
like an old branch upon a great oak tree?"

                                  So, therefore, what          120
then is to be read tenderly and with a languid neck:
*torva mimalloneis inplerunt cornua bombis,*
*et raptum vitulo caput ablatura superbo*
*Bassaris et lyncem Mœnas flexura corymbis*
*euhion ingeminat, reparabilis adsonat echo?*          125
Would these be performed if any vein of a paternal
testicle were alive in us? This weak stuff swims atop
saliva upon the lips and thrives on drivel, Mænas
and Attis, and neither does it belabor the writing
desk nor smell of bitten fingernails.          130

                    "But why is there need
to scratch sensitive ears with truth? Be careful, if you will,
lest the doorsteps of great ones become by chance cold to you;
hereupon the canine letter sounds from the nose."

                                      Indeed,          135
let everything from now on be lovely, for all I care.
I'll get in no one's way. Everything, everything will be
rightly marvelous. Is this helpful? You say, "I forbid

---

[7] Practice of begging sailors.

[8] *i.e.,* Virgil's Æneid.

anyone here who defecates." Paint two snakes, boys, the place
is sacred, piss outside!                                          140

          I'm leaving. Lucilius cut
up the City, you Lupus, you Mucius, and he broke
his jaw tooth on them. Let into the circus, Flaccus[9] probes
and mocks every fault, every passion for his laughing friends;
skillfully suspending the people from his brandished nose.        145
Wrong for me to mumble? Not secretly, nor with a ditch?
Nowhere? Yet I shall dig a ditch here. I have seen, I myself have seen,
little book—*who has not the ears of an ass?* This
secret, this my laughter so futile, I offer to sell
to you whoever inspired by the outspoken Cratinus,[10]            150
not by said Iliad,[11] pales with the grand old man[12] over
angry Eupolis; look at these my words if, by chance,
you listen for something much boiled down. Let my reader be
one who, his ear thereby incensed, seethes with indignation,
not this vile man who enjoys making fun of the sandals            155
of Greeks, and who can call a man with one eye by the name
"one eye," believing himself something because, puffed up by
Italian honor, he has broken short half-pint measures
as the Ædile of Arretium; nor the crafty man
who has the conceit to laugh at the abacus numbers               160
and the cones drawn in the sand, ready to be overjoyed
if a lewd trull pulls the beard of a cynic; I give these
the playbill in the morn, after dinner, Calliroen.

---

[9] The Roman poet Quintus Horatius Flaccus, known as Horace.

[10] Representative, with Eupolis, *infra*, of fifth-century Athenian Comedy.

[11] Vid. Lines 61-62, *supra*.

[12] Lucilius, Roman poet, credited with conception of Roman satire.

# SATIRE II

## SUMMARY OF SATIRE II

Persius satirizes worshippers whose prayers, unheard by others and made to the gods, would scandalize a scoundrel if made to him; and warns such prayers cannot be made with impunity (lines 1-37). He rejects silly prayers made on behalf of others (lines 38-49), scoffs at worshippers whose conduct is inconsistent with the results sought in their prayers (lines 49-64), and chides earthly beings for their delusion that the gods will be moved to act favorably by the introduction into the temples of practices that satisfy our standards of worth (lines 65-84). Persius concludes by describing the offering he believes the gods favor (lines 85-90).

## SATIRE II VERSE

*Number this day, Macrinus*, with the lucky stone, the one
colored white, which marks for you the years as they pass you by.
Pour out the wine for your genius. You do not haggle in
your prayers asking for what you can only disclose in
confidence to the gods; but a large part of the wealthy                    5
will go on offering libations with muffled censers.
It is not easy for just anyone to discard their
murmurs and humble whispers from the temples and live with
an open prayer. "May my mind, credit, repute be good."
These sorts of things he says clearly that a stranger may hear;            10
other sorts he murmurs inward to himself and unheard:
"O, if my uncle would pass on, a splendid funeral!"
and "O, if a jar of silver would rattle under my
rake with the help of Hercules' right hand, or would that I
might strike out my ward whom I, as next of kin, would replace.           15
Indeed, he is scabby and swells with acute bile. A third
wife is already taken by Nerius!" So that you
may piously pray for these things, in the Tiber's stream you
dip your head two and three times in the early morning and
thus you purify the taintings in the flowing water.                       20
Ho, come, answer, what I want to know is very little—
what do you feel about Jove? Is there one above whom you

9

care to put Jove? "Above whom?" Yes, above whom. Do you wish
Statius?[13] Or, do I sense you are reluctant? Who is
a better judge or more suitable for orphan children?[14]                     25
Therefore, this with which you try to reach the ear of Jove, then
say to Statius. "O, Jupiter!" he would shout. "O, gracious
Jupiter!" But would not Jupiter himself do his own
shouting? Do you think he has overlooked you because when
he thunders, the oak tree is sooner shattered by the sacred           30
bolt than you or your home? Or because you are not lying,
ordained by the soothsayer Ergenna and the entrails
of her sheep, in a wooded spot made sacred by your fall,
a sad victim to be avoided. Is that the reason
Jupiter offers you his silly beard to pull? Or what                          35
then is it—at what price do you purchase the ears of the
gods? With a lung and greasy guts?

                      Behold, a grandmother
or a maternal aunt, fearful of the gods, lifts the child
from his cradle and purifies his wet little lips with                          40
her middle finger moistened with her cleansing saliva,
she being skilled to prevent the evil eye; then she shakes
him in her hands and anticipates in a suppliant prayer
the slim hope now in the fields of Licinus, now in the
halls of Crassus. "May the rich man and his wife choose this one      45
for a son-in-law! May the young girls chase this one! Let
roses spring up wherever this one has walked!" But I do
not entrust prayers to a nurse; refuse her, Jupiter,
in however much white[15] she will have pled.

                      You ask support      50
for your vigor and a body lasting to old age. So
be it; but great dishes and thick sausages have forbid
the gods to assent to these requests; and they do confound
propitious Jupiter.

---

[13] Probably a well-known scoundrel who mistreats his ward(s).

[14] Sarcasm.

[15] Proper attire for worshippers.

You wish to create riches by                                        55
sacrificing oxen and you summon Mercury with
entrails. "Bless me, household deities, give me a herd and
increases to my flocks!" On what terms, O worst of men, when
so many entrails of your young oxen melt away in
the flames? And still this man struggles to succeed, offering        60
up entrails and rich cakes. "Now my field increases," he cries,
"now the sheepfold increases, now it will be granted, now,
now!" until begilded and in despair, in the bottom of
the chest his last coin sighs, "In vain."

                       If I were to give you               65
bowls of silver embossed with thick gold, you would sweat and your
heart palpitating with happiness would exude drops down
your left breast. From this it has come to pass that you smear the
sacred features with triumphal gold; for "among brazen
brothers, those who send dreams most cleansed of humors, let them   70
be the foremost and have the golden beard." Gold has pushed out the
vases of Numa and the Saturnian bronze, and gold
takes the place of Vestal urns and Etruscan earthenware.
O, bent earthbound spirits and empty of heavenly instincts,
what help is this—to send our customs into the temples            75
and infer good things for the gods from this our sinful flesh?
This flesh dissolves cassia to its taste though the olive
oil is thereby spoiled, this flesh boils Calabian wool in
corrupted[16] purple dye, this flesh demands the pearl be torn
from its shell and veins of seething metal be stripped out of      80
the crude earth. And this flesh does sin, it does sin; nonetheless
it makes use of its sin. But you, holy men, tell us, what
does gold bring about in a holy place? Just as much, to
be sure, as a doll given to Venus by a virgin.[17]

Give we rather to the gods what the blear-eyed offspring of        85
Messalla could not give from his huge platter: justice and
compassion together in the soul, incorruptible

---

[16] By the boiling of the wool.

[17] Virtually nothing.

11

recesses of the mind and a heart imbued with noble
virtue. Let me take these to the temples and I will make
my sacrifice with a handful of grain. 95

# SATIRE III

---

## SUMMARY OF SATIRE III

The protagonist of this sermon is a young man of good estate and family who refuses to establish worthwhile goals and apply himself to them (lines 1-65). Persius urges him to follow philosophic remedies (lines 66-77), reminding him that only a fool would ignore this advice (lines 78-89) and that remedies for bodily sickness are useless to him (lines 90-123).

## SATIRE III VERSE

*"So this is always the state of things?* Already the clear
morning is coming in the windows and lengthening in
its light the shutter chinks. We[18] are snoring what should suffice
to get rid of the potent Falernian wine, while the
line of the dial is touched by the fifth shadow. Look at you!          5
Now for a while the mad dog star has been parching the crops
and all of the herd has been beneath the spreading elm tree."
One of his companions is speaking. "Is it so? Is it?
Get someone in here quickly. Is there no one? My glassy
bile is beginning to swell—I'm about to burst!" Just like, you          10
would say, the Arcadian herds of cattle would bellow.
Now the book and smooth two-colored parchment and papyrus,
also a knotty reed, have come into his hands. Then we
complain because the thick fluid hangs onto the pen but
the black color fades when water is added; we          15
complain when the pen doubles the flow of the diluted
drops. Wretched youth, and more wretched in the days to come,
have we come to this state of things? Ah, why don't you, rather
like a soft dove and the boys of the rich, demand a bit piece
to eat and, infuriated, reject the lullaby          20
of the nurse? "Can I apply myself with a pen like this?"
To whom are you talking? Why are you chirping foolishness?
You are only amusing yourself; you are losing touch

---

[18] Use of "we" in lines 3, 13, 15, and 18: sarcastic belittling use of "we" in speaking of one who is misbehaving like a child.

and you know better; you will be contemned.

*Improve Yourself*

                                             The ill-baked jar  25
of green clay sounds the fault when struck and responds grudgingly.
You are moist and pliant clay; now, now you must hasten and
be thoroughly refashioned upon the sharp wheel. But you
have at your paternal countryside a supply of wheat, a
pure and spotless salt cellar and a dish free of want as         30
your fireside guardian. "Therefore," you ask, "what should I fear?"
Is this enough? Or would it be fitting to fill your lung
with air until it bursts because you descend, thousandth branch,
from an Etruscan family tree or greet your Censor,
or because you greet him as a knight? Your trappings to the    35
mob! I have known you inside and out. Is it not shameful
to live in the manner of loose-living Natta? But this
man is stupefied from vice and a thick fat has grown on
his heart; he can't be blamed, he does not know what he loses,
and sunk in the deep he no more bubbles on the water's     40
surface.

                 Often as a small boy, I remember, I touched
my eyes with oil if I wished not to learn Cato's sublime
words as he was about to die (words which must be greatly
praised by the crazy teacher) so that my sweating father    45
might hear them with friends he brought along. That was me; indeed
the foremost concern in my prayers was to know what the
lucky six would bring, how much the damned aces would erase,
that I would not be faulted by the neck of the narrow
jar and none would be more skilled than I with the thong-whipped top.
But by no means are you now unprepared to comprehend
deviant habits and what the wise Porch (whereon trousered
Persians are scribbled) teaches, over which young men, sleepy
and unshorn, stay awake fed by edible seeds and much
porridge; and the letter which stretched apart the Samian    55
arms has shown you the path which rises along the right side.

*Do Not Delay Further*

Are you still snoring? The head, suffering from yesterday,
is still and relaxed, the neck loosened, the unhampered
jaws wide open. Is there anything for which you stretch out
and toward which you aim your bow? Or are you pursuing          60
ravens with brick and mud and no direction, content with
where your foot carries you and living for just the moment?
One sees men asking for hellebore in vain when the sick skin
will already be swollen, hasten to meeting approaching
illness, and what need to promise great piles to Craterus.[19]   65

*The Way Is Knowledge*

Learn, O wretched men, and know the causes of things: what we
are and what then we are born to accomplish; what order
given and where the turn around the goal is smooth and whence
begun; what limit upon money; what is right to choose;
what useful has the new coin; how much is proper to be          70
given to your country and to dear relatives; whom has
the god ordered you to be and where in the human race
have you been placed. Learn, and do not be envious[20] because
many a pot goes bad in a well-stocked storeroom after
the wealthy Umbrians have been defended, and pepper            75
and hams, reminders of the Marsian clients; and the
fish has not yet been emptied from the first jar.

*Some People Pay No Attention*[21]

At this point, someone of the smelly Centurion clan
might say: "What I know is enough for me. I don't intend
to be what Arciselas and the trouble-making Solons            80
intend while, head bent down and fixing on the ground with their
eyes, they chew over murmurs mixed with maddening silence
and weigh their words on a protruded lip, meditating

---

[19] A doctor.
[20] Cf. *Satire IV*, lines 15-20.
[21] Cf. St. Matthew, Chap. 13, v. 4

over the dreams of some sick old man: *nothing is created
from nothing, nothing can be turned into nothing.* Is this                85
what you turn pale over? Is this why anyone would miss
a meal?" The people are amused by these remarks and the
hefty young men double the tremulous laughter with their
noses curling.

*Symptoms of Bodily Sickness*

                    "Look me over; I don't know why my chest            90
palpitates and a foul odor comes from my weak throat;
take a look, if you will!" He is speaking to the doctor
who, ordered to rest, after the third night has seen the veins
run smoothly, has asked from a rich house a smooth Surrentine
wine in a moderately thirsting bottle for himself                         95
on his way to the bath. "Hey, good man, you look pale." "It is
nothing." "Nevertheless, you should check this out, whatever
it is, you are not aware your skin is turning yellow."
"But you are turning pale in a worst way; do not be my
guardian. I buried him some time ago; you remain."                       100
"Go about your business, I'll say no more." This man swollen
from eating and with a pale stomach goes about his bath,
while his throat slowly exhales sulfurous vapors; but a
trembling comes upon his limbs and he drops his warm tumbler
from his hand, his exposed teeth chatter, then from his relaxed         105
lips fall oily relishes. Thereupon trumpet, candles
and at last the blessed man, placed on a lofty couch and
smeared with a thick ointment, points his stiff legs toward the door.
Moreover, yesterday's slaves wearing their caps of newfound
freedom are the ones who lift him up and carry him out.                 110

*You Are Sick Not in Body But in Mind and Spirit*

Wretched youth,[22] touch your veins and put your right hand on your
breast, no fever here; touch your extremities, feet and hands,
they are not cold. But if by chance some money is seen or if
a fair girl of the neighborhood has softly smiled, does your

---

[22] The "wretched youth" in line 17 and addressed in line 73.

heart, as I would expect, leap a bit? On a cold plate, a        115
rough vegetable is put before you and flour of the
people is shaken from the sieve. Let us try your jaws. A
putrid lesion lies hidden in your tender mouth, which a
plebian beet may not be fitting to graze. Cold you are,[23]
whenever pale fear[24] has raised the hairs from your arms and legs.    120
Now, with a torch[25] placed beneath, the blood begins to boil and
the eyes sparkle with anger, and you say and do that which
insane Orestes himself would swear is not a sane man's.[26]

---

[23] Not cold in fact, but in the context of sickness of the mind and spirit.

[24] Resulting from the discovery of the putrid sore in the mouth, or otherwise.

[25] Whatever provokes you. The image is an angry man as a boiling kettle.

[26] In lines 78-123, Persius is saying, in conclusion, to the wretched young man of line 17: unless you are one who will pay no attention to what I say (lines 78-89), listen when I tell you that you are not sick in body (lines 90-113) but in mind and spirit (lines 1-24, 57-62, 113-123); and you must follow my advice (lines 25-77) to be cured.

# CONCERNING THE PUNISHMENT OF TYRANTS[27]

*Great father of the gods,* let it be your wish to punish
harsh tyrants in no other manner when cruel self-will,
imbued with seething poison, has produced a sinister
effect on the natural disposition: let them see
virtue and waste away at the sight they have forsaken.                    5
Have the bronze Sicilian bulls groaned with more pain and has
the sword hanging from the golden panelled ceilings stricken
the neck beneath bedecked in purple with more foreboding
than if one to himself bemoans, "I am going, I am
going head long down," and within he turns pale with fear which      10
even one so close as his dear wife fails to recognize.

---

[27] A separate satire but tucked away in *Satire III*, between lines 41 and 42, *supra*, probably
to lessen the risk of an affront to the Emperor.

# SATIRE IV

## SUMMARY OF SATIRE IV

Satire IV contains a medley of satires: the first satirizes both Greek philosophers for their ignorance and politicians who must be able to sell a bill of goods to be successful (lines 1-24); the second satirizes miserly rich men and the people who look disparagingly at them rather than into themselves (lines 25-35); and the third pictures a clever homosexual promoting his preference of sexual practices (lines 36-45). In conclusion, Persius restates his philosophy of self-knowledge also set forth in Satire I, line 8 and Satire VI, lines 28-29 (lines 46-58).

## SATIRE IV VERSE

A MEDLEY

"But I am a scoffer with a saucy sense of humor."

*—Satire I, line 14*

*The Sense Every Politician Needs*

"Are you handling the affairs of government?" Imagine
the bearded teacher to say these words, whom a fatal dose
of hemlock has taken away. "Relying upon what?
Tell me this, pupil of great Pericles. Obviously
genius and a quick grasp of matters have reached you before          5
a beard, you understand what must be said and be not said.
Therefore, when the rabble rage, moved by anger, you press
to bring about silence of the heated multitude by
the majesty of your hand. What will you say? 'Regard
this, Citizens, as unjust, judge that badly, that rightly.'          10
Indeed, you know to weigh what is just on a tray of the
two-trayed balance, you distinguish what is straight when it comes
among what is crooked, or when the rule deceives with a
diverse foot, and you can mark a fault with the black theta.
Therefore, why don't you, lovely in appearance though you are,          15
cease before your allotted time tossing your tail in vain
before the caressing people, being more fit for the
pure hellebore of the philosopher. What in your judgment
is the greatest good? To have lived, you say, constantly with

a dish of rich food and with your skin cared for in the sun.          20
Now, hold it, this old woman would not otherwise answer.
Go now, roar 'I'm Dinomache's son, I'm captivating.'"

He shall be, provided he has not less sense than shriveled
Baucis peddling to the unwary greens meant for a slave.

## A View of the Rich Man

How few try to descend into their own bosoms, nobody          25
indeed, but the wallet on the back preceding is watched!
Should you have asked, "Are you familiar with the estate of
Vetidius?" "Whose?" "The wealthy man who plows at Cures
more than a kite can cover." "This man you are speaking of,
this man, plagued by the angry gods and his perverse nature,          30
who, whenever he hangs up the yoke at the Festival
of Compitalia, fearing to scrape off the mold of
his little bottle, sighs, 'To your health!' eating an onion
layer by layer with salt and, while his slaves applaud their
corn mess,[28] drinks the ragged dregs of the dying vinegar?"          35

## Man to Man

And should you be resting with your body oiled and fix the
sunlight on your skin, there's sure to be a stranger nearby
who would touch you with his sharp elbow and say with a lisp:
"Today's trends! Weeding out the penis and the loin's hidden
secrets to make the gaping genitals more popular!          40
Since you comb a perfumed thicket on your jaws, have you been
barbered there whereby your worm is poking out from your groin?
Granted, wrestlers may pull on these saplings five times with curved
forceps and make firm buttocks tremble; this fern patch of yours,
however, does not soften no matter how often plowed."          45

## Know Thyself

We strike down, and in turn we show our legs to the arrows.
Life is lived under those conditions—so we have known. Beneath

---

[28] A meal which other laborers get every day.

the groin you have a hidden wound, but the girdle covers
it in front with a broad bit of gold. As you wish, pretend
otherwise and overestimate your strength, if you can.                    50
"When my neighbor calls me outstanding, should I not believe?"
If, perverse one, you turn pale at the sight of money, if
you make whatever love comes your way into just a sport,
if you whip, being careful, the business world with many
blows, you will have given for no purpose your thirsting ears              55
to the people. Spit it out, what you are not; let Cerdo
take away what he has provided. Live with yourself, find
out how the abbreviated furniture does suit you.[29]

---

[29] Cf. *Satire I*, line 8; *Satire VI*, lines 28-9.

# SATIRE V

## SUMMARY OF SATIRE V

Satire V opens with a satire of certain poets (lines 1-15). Persius follows with a tribute to his friend and teacher Cornutus (lines 16-55), whose teachings he urges his men to follow (lines 56-79); and a philosophic discussion of freedom (lines 80-141) and the masters within, which must be overcome if men are to enjoy freedom (lines 142-227), including avarice (lines 151-164), luxury (lines 164-177), infatuation (lines 187-206), ambition (lines 207-212), and superstition (lines 213-227).

## SATIRE V VERSE

*This is the custom of the poets,* to demand for themselves
one hundred voices, to insist on one hundred mouths and tongues
for their songs, whether a written tale must be poured forth by
the gaping tragic actor or about wounds inflicted
on the Parthian trying to draw the dart from his groin.              5
"For what purpose these voices? Or how large are the lumps of
robust poetry you pour in so that your song is up to
exerting one hundred throats? Let those who pompously will
speak gather fluffiness from Helicon, whoever will
set to boiling the pot of Procne or Thyestes[30] whose              10
fare Glyco[31] must often eat, mindless of the taste. Neither
do you press the wind from the panting bellows until the
ore is refined in the fire; nor caw hoarsely like a crow
to yourself some weighty trash in a restrained murmuring;
nor do you stretch the swollen cheeks to burst with a *stloppo.*     15
You adopt the language of everyday life, skilled to make
keen comparisons and to polish your verse with temperate
expression, learned to scratch decadent practices raw
and to fix fault with delicate play. From this draw what you
say, and leave the tragic meals with their gory heads and feet to    20
Mycenae; and get to know the meals of common people."

---

[30] Common tragic themes on Rome as well as Athens. Procne served up her son and Thyestes made a dinner of his.

[31] A stupid actor.

I strive not for this, that my page swell with bubbly stuff and
make from smoke seeming substance. We are talking privately.
Now, encouraged by the Muse, I am expressing to you
innermost feelings that I feel compelled to lay open;                    25
and it gives me joy, Cornutus, to uncover for you,
sweet friend, how much a part of my soul does belong to you.
Strike, careful to distinguish what sounds solid and stucco
made of the painted tongue. In this cause I would dare demand
one hundred voices that I may make known in uncolored            30
sound how firmly I have fixed you in my entwining breast
and the words may liberate all of this which is hidden,
unable to be spoken by the heart, which has no tongue.

When first the guardian purple left me in fear and the
boyhood boss hung dedicated to the girded hearth gods,           35
when flattering companions and the toga's now white knot
permitted me to cast my eyes safely over all the
Subura; and when the way became uncertain, and my
wandering about, ignorant of life, led my anxious
mind to the branching crossroads, I threw myself upon you       40
as a son, and you accepted my tender years, Cornutus,
in your Socratic bosom. Then your beguiling ruler
applied to my distorted ways straightens them, and my mind
is pressed by reason and endeavors to be overcome;
and takes on the countenance as fashioned under your thumb.   45
And I remember passing long days with you, and with you
plucking early evenings for our meals. We both arrange to
work and rest alike and relieve our cares at a modest
table. Indeed you must not doubt this: the days of both are
in harmony by a sure compact and let by one star.                    50
Whether, perceiving this truth, Parca[32] hangs our lives by the
level Balance[33] or Hora[34] divides between the Twins[35] two

---

[32] The goddess who allots his fate to each.
[33] The Zodiac figure consisting of two-tray scales in perfect balance.
[34] One of the Horæ whose functions extended to the events of human life.

concordant destinies made fit for faithful friends, and we
together, aided by our Jove, master grim Saturn,[36] I
know not. What is certain is that a star blends me with you.          55

Men see things in a thousand different ways and their use of
what they have has many colors. Each one has his own choices,
and no one purpose guides our lives. This man sells his wrinkled
pepper and seeds of pale cumin in the early morning
for Italian goods; this man prefers, after a full meal,          60
to swell up in a refreshing sleep; this man gives himself
up to politics; gambling lays waste to this man; that man
wastes away for love; but when disabling gout has shattered
the fingers like branches of an old beech tree, then, too late,
they have sighed to themselves that the days have passed by joyless,          65
their splendor obscured; and over the life they have foregone.

But you take delight in growing pale over nightly papers,
for you plant Cleanthean virtue in young men's cleansed ears.
Seek from this, young and old, sure discipline for the spirit
and comfort for a piteous old age! "Tomorrow this          70
will be done." Tomorrow the same will be said. "What? Do you
really talk of one day as if it makes a difference?"
But when the next day has come, we have now brought to an end
yesterday's tomorrow. See how one tomorrow after
another bears away these years of ours and will always          75
be a little out of reach. For, ever so close to you,
although turning under one and the same wagon, you will
try to catch the wheel in vain when you are the wheel behind
and running on the following axle.

*Concerning Freedom*

                                        This freedom is not          80
needed: freedom whereby, as each Publius enters his
service in the Veline tribe, he possesses by means of

---

[35] The Zodiac figure consisting of two human forms which are mirror images of each other.

[36] Representing life's obstacles.

a ticket some moldy grain. Alas, empty of meaning
the proceedings by which a twirl makes one a citizen!
This Damus is a worthless stable boy, blear eyed from cheap     85
wine and apt to lie about a bit of fodder. Should the
master turn him around, from the impulse of the twirling
he goes forth as Marcus Dama. Wonderful! What's this? Though
Marcus is surety, are you refusing to make the
loan; thrown to the mercy of Judge Marcus, are you turning     90
pale with anxiety? Marcus speaks: so it is. Marcus,
put your hand and seal to the documents. This is freedom
in name only. This is what the liberty caps give us.

"Or is anyone else free unless it is permitted
him to lead his life as he wishes? It is permitted     95
that I live as I wish. Am I not more free than Brutus?"
"You conclude falsely," says the Stoic at this point, having
washed his ears with sharp vinegar,[37] "I accept what remains,[38]
take away *it is permitted* and *as I wish*." "After
I have returned from the Praetor, made my own man by his     100
wand of freedom, why is whatever my will commands not
permitted me, except whatever the Masurian
statutes forbid?"

       Learn, but remove the pique and that mocking
grimace from your nose while I pull from your breast old mothers'   105
tales. It was not the Praetor's role to give fools a refined
sense of duty for affairs or to cast out to them the
full practice of consuming life. You would sooner fit the
harp to a hulking drudge. Reason opposes it and whispers
privately in the ear that no one should be permitted     110
to do that which he will do faultily. Nature and the
general law of mankind adhere to this commandment:

---

[37] The preceding argument is essentially in the same form as: All fathers are men, therefore all men are fathers; and its conclusion, says the Stoic, invalid (though not necessarily false).

[38] The Stoic proceeds to the substance of his argument and denies both that man has a will and that he is free to follow it.

that feeble ignorance must refrain from such actions as
forbidden. Do you dilute hellebore not knowing how to
fix the tongue of the scale at the point of balance? This the          115
nature of healing forbids. If a country bumpkin would
demand a ship for himself, ignorant of the pole star,
the sailor's patron would shout that modesty had perished
from the world. Has philosophy taught you to live so that
you do not stumble, and do you have the experience          120
to distinguish the truth's appearance lest something rings false,
the gold only gilding the copper beneath? Have you marked
both what should be followed and what should be avoided, in
turn, those with white, then these with black? Are you moderate in
your prayers, spiteless to friends when you beseech the house gods?   125

Would you stuff your warehouse full, would you promptly empty it
(making a large profit), and would you be able to step
over the coin fixed in the dirt and not swallow like a
glutton the trader's saliva?[39] When you will have truly
said, "These are mine, I know," be then free by the grace of the          130
Praetor and propitious Jove. But, although you may have
been a little earlier of my persuasion, if you
retain your old skin and, cleansed on the forehead, yet shelter
in your blemished heart a crafty fox, I will gather up
whatI had offered you above and I draw back the lifeline.          135
Philosophy has bestowed nothing on you; thrust out your
finger, you are sinning, and what is such a trifle? But
you will be sacrificing in vain to cause a brief speck
of sense to stick in fools. It is wrong to mix these; and if
you are otherwise a ditch digger, you would not dance so          140
much as three steps of the Satyric dance of Bathyllus.

*The Masters Within*

"I am free." Whence do you feel that is given, you who are
under so many controls. Or are you unaware of
any master except whom the wand has removed? "Go, slave, and

---

[39] Cf. *Satire VI*, lines 91-97.

take the scrappers to the baths of Crispinus!" If he scolds: 145
"Trifler, are you dawdling?" no sharp servitude moves you and
nothing outside of yourself sets you into action; but,
if within and in a sick heart, masters are born, how do
you escape with more impunity than he whom whipping
and fear of the master drives to the scrappers? 150
                              Early in
the morning and you are lazily snoring. "Get up," says
Avarice. "Come on, get up!" You refuse. She presses on.
"Get up," she says. "I cannot." "Get up." "And what shall I do?"
"You ask! Come, carry fish from the Pontus, oakum, 155
aromatics, ebony, incense, and smooth Coan wine;
be the first to unload fresh pepper from the thirsty camel;
do some business, conspire." "But Jupiter will be listening."
"Alas, blockhead, you must go through life content to bore a
hole with your finger in the often tasted salt cellar,[40] 160
if you propose to live with Jove." Already you are well
equipped and getting skin and wine casks ready for the slaves.
"Quickly to the ship!" Nothing stands in the way but that you
scour the Aegean in your huge ship except Luxury
warns you, having been first taken aside: "Where are you rushing 165
next, insane man? Where? What do you want for yourself? Has a
compelling madness boiled up beneath your overwrought breast
which gallons of hemlock will not have cured? You would hasten
over the sea, your meal on a rower's bench, you propped on
a coil of rope and a broad bottom bottle breaths forth poor 170
red wine impaired by moldy pitch? What are you looking for?
That funds you had nourished here at a modest five percent
would go on to sweat out a greedy eleven percent?
Attend to yourself. Let us pluck off what are the sweet things.
You are living when you follow me. Ashes and shade 175
and a tale you will become. Live mindful of death; time flies.
This which I am speaking comes out of it."

---

[40] To live sparsely.

Come, what are you

doing? You are being torn in different directions.

Is it this way or that way you follow? It behooves you          180

to approach your masters in turn with seeming submission,

in turn stray away from them. And, when you have once stood firm

and refused to obey a pressing command, you must not

say, "Now I have broken my chains"; for a dog also with

a struggle breaks his knot loose, and yet when he flees a          185

long piece of his chain is dragged from his collar.

"Believe this,

Davus, no question about it, I am thinking about

putting an end to the torments I have been going through,"

Chaerestratus says this, chewing on bloody fingernails.          190

"Whether I should be standing as a disgrace before my

sober relatives; whether I should be wasting away,

as some base reports would have it, my paternal estate

outside a bawdy house while I am drunk and singing in

front of Chrysis's dripping doors with a doused torch." "Well said,          195

young sir; you should know the right choice, sacrifice the lamb to

the gods who look over us." "But do you not think, Davus,

she will weep over being abandoned?" "You are talking

nonsense; she will scold, young sir, with the red slipper, so that

you desire to waver no longer and to gnaw the tight          200

net now madly like a wild animal." "But if she calls,

tell me right now what, therefore, shall I do; and when she calls

and begs besides, should I not now go to her?" "If you have

escaped complete and whole from that—not now." Here, here is what

we are looking for, not in the wand which the Lictor casts          205

about to no avail.

Is that flattering candidate

his own master whom chalked Ambitio[41] drags about, his

mouth agape with yearning? Get up early, you, and cast chick

peas bounteously among the factious people so that          210

old men lolling in the sun can recall our Festival

---

[41] The goddess of canvassing.

of Flora. Is anything more noble?[42]

                          But when Herod's
days have come and lamps bearing violets in the oily
window set have poured forth their thick cloud and the tail of the   215
tunny fish, as if swimming, has embraced the red serving
dish, the white jug bulges with wine: then you move your lips in
silence and turn pale with fear of the circumcised Sabbath.
Then black spectors and dangers promised by the burst egg shell.
Then huge priests of Cybele and the one-eyed priestess with her   220
timbrel have excited the gods who puff up bodies if
you have not tasted three times in the early morning the
prescribed head of garlic.

                     When you have said these things among
the straddling centurions, great Puffennius at once             225
laughs gruffly and offers a clipped cent for one hundred Greek
philosophers.

---

[42] Sarcastic reference to specious self-mastering of the candidate who is dominated by Ambitio.

# SATIRE VI

## SUMMARY OF SATIRE VI

This satire is a medley consisting of a warm greeting to his friend Bassus (lines 1-24), a satire of a stingy man with a specious reason not to help a friend in need, in which Persius reinforces the point by hoisting himself on his own petard (lines 30-62); a satire on those who inflate the importance of ancestry (lines 63-73); a satire on a man who enjoys an extravagant lifestyle and tries to keep his heir from asking too many questions about his inheritance (lines 74-90); and a satire of the man of commerce who says he is willing to stop accumulating riches (lines 91-97).

## SATIRE VI VERSE

A MEDLEY

*Greetings to Bassus*

Bassus, has the winter moved you now to your Sabine hearth?
Now by your exacting touch are strings and lyre come alive?
Artisan superb, so skilled to join the ancient voices
with the manly measures of the Latin harp, then youthful
frolics to excite and make a sport of old age with your          5
gracious and uncommon thumb. The Ligurian coast now
warms me and my sea is wintering where rocky huge cliffs
provide me the shore and the coast withdraws to a deep bay.
"Citizens, the port of Luna come to know; it's worthwhile."
So demands Ennius from his heart, when he's done snoring—       10
dreaming that he's the fifth Homer in the peacock's order.
I'm here free of public bother, also from what troubles
for my herd the south wind plans, and it does not bother me
that my neighbor's corner there is more fruitful than mine own.
Even if everyone born beneath me should become rich,             15
I would, when stooped with old age, refute that I have bent at
all because of that or ate a tasteless meal and have touched
with my nose the seal on a bottle of insipid wine.
Another may disagree with what I say. Horoscope,
you give birth to twins of different dispositions: there is       20

one who only on his birthday moistens his bone dry greens
with brine he bought stingily by the cup, and he himself
sprinkles precious pepper on the plate; over here in spirits
high a youth devours great possessions without self restraint.
I shall enjoy life; and to that end I shall have no need                    25
to put elegantly before my slaves the turbot fish
nor appreciate the delicate spittle of the thrush.
Live within your own harvest and grind out your granary;
this is right. What do you fear? Just plow, a new crop comes forth.

## Persius' Effort to Ridicule

But duty calls and a friend, his ship shattered, hangs helpless          30
on distant rocks, having buried all his cargo with his
unheard prayers in the Ionian Sea. The master
lies on shore and with him large gods painted on the transom,
and ribs of the broken vessel now attracting sea birds.
Well now, break off something from your fertile turf, give to the        35
needy lest he roam about painted on a sea green plank.
But your heir, angered thereby, will neglect your funeral feast
because you have stunted your estate, and he will commit your
ashes badly flavored to the urn, resolved not to know
if the cinnamon exhales scent or the cassia bark                          40
goes astray with the cherry. Would you be out of harm's way
diminishing your estate?[43]

            Moreover, Bestius scolds
the Greek teachers: "It so happens, since this wholesome taste[44] of
ours came with pepper and dates to the city, the rustic                  45
laborers have been spoiling their porridges with a thick
and fatty sauce." Would you fear such a state of affairs on
account of your ashes when you are on the other side?[45]

## Persius Hoist on His Own Petard

But you, whoever will be my heir, a little removed

---

[43] Asked with tongue in cheek.

[44] Sarcasm.

[45] Asked with tongue in cheek.

from the crowd, listen.[46] O good man, have you not heard? A bay-      50
bound letter has been sent by Cæsar resulting from the
notable slaughter of the German youth[47] and cold ashes
are shaken from the altars, and now Cæsonia is
placing arms for the temple gates, now cloaks for kings, now wigs
of yellow for the captives, wagons and huge Rhinelanders.      55

Therefore, because of matters admirably accomplished
by the gods and our leader's genius,[48] I'm bringing in one
hundred pairs of gladiators;[49] who forbids? I dare you!
Woe to you if you do not allow it! I am giving
oil and bread and meat to the rabble. Or do you forbid?      60
Speak clearly! "The ashes," you say, "needed for that have not
been cleared from the nearby field; go get them."

*Speaking of Heirs*

　　　　　　　　　　If I have no
survivors of my paternal aunts, no descendants of
my father's brother, no great granddaughter of my uncle      65
remains, my maternal aunt has died childless, and from my
grandmother none survives, I am going to Bovillæ, to
the slope of Virbius: Manius my heir is at hand.
"A groundling?" you ask. Ask me who is my great great grandfather;
not quickly, but I will name him; add one generation      70
and still another: now there is a groundling, and now by
ritual of descent this Manius turns out to be
my near great granduncle.

*Feigned Resentment To End An Awkward Inquiry*

　　　　　　　　　　You who are in front of me,[50] why
do you demand the torch from me before I can reach you?      75
I am your Mercury; like the god I come hither as

---

[46] A mock confrontation follows.

[47] Sarcasm.

[48] Sarcasm.

[49] A costly exhibition.

[50] Image is life as a relay race.

he is pictured with a purse. Are you willing to enjoy
what remains or are you nodding your head "no"? Something is
missing from the whole amount. I reduced it for myself
but all is yours, whatever it is. Do not ask where is                         80
what Tadius had left me some time ago, and do not
bring up my father's advice to me: that my expenses must
not be greater than the amount of the interest I earn.[51]
"So," you ask, "how much is left?" How much is left, did you say?
Now, now, boy, smear the cabbages extravagantly. On a               85
feast day shall nettles be cooked for me and a smoked pig's
head with sliced ears, so that at some future time this spendthrift
of yours, full of goose, while his vein throbs within his fickle
wandering _____, _____ into a classy _____ ? Would the woof
of a shape be mine, but a priest's fat stomach shakes for him?      90

### Invective Against Men of Commerce

Sell your soul for money, trade and search every side of the
world, and there is not another better suited to slap
fat Cappadocian slaves on the trader's platform; double
your money. "I have done that, already three times, now for
the fourth time, already for the tenth time it returns to              95
my purse. Prick me when I should stop." Found, the man to
put a limit to your heap,[52] Chrysippus.

---

[51] Because Tadius' legacy has been spent and the father's advice has been ignored in extravagant living.

[52] Such a man does not exist.

# Original

*Latin*

# SATURA I

'O curas hominum! O quantum est in rebus inane!
Quis leget haec?
      'Min tu istud ais? Nemo hercule.'
          Nemo?                           5
'Vel duo, vel nemo.'
        Turpe et miserabile!
         'Quare?
ne mihi Polydamas et Troiades Labeonem
praetulerint? nugae. non, si quid turbida Roma          10
elevet, accedas examenque improbum in illa
castiges trutina, nec te quaesiveris extra.
nam Romae quis non--? a, si fas dicere—sed fas
tum, cum ad canitiem et nostrum istud vivere triste
aspexi ac nucibus facimus quaecumque relictis,         15
cum sapimus patruos. Tunc, tunc ignoscite.'
        Nolo.
'Quid faciam? sed sum petulanti splene cachinno.
  Scribimus inclusi, numeros ille, hic pede liber,
grande aliquid, quod pulmo animae praelargus anhelet.    20
scilicet haec populo pexusque togaque recenti
et natalicia tandem cum sardonyche albus
sede leges celsa, liquido cum plasmate guttur
mobile collueris, patranti fractus ocello.
hic neque more probo videas nec voce serena         25
ingentis trepidare Titos, cum carmina lumbum
intrant, et tremulo scalpuntur ubi intima versu.
tun, vetule, auriculis alienis colligis escas,
auriculis, quibus et dicas cute perditus olie?'
  Quo didicisse, nisi hoc fermentum et quae semel intus   30
innata est rupto iecore exierit caprificus?
    'En pallor seniumque! O mores! usque adeone
scire tuum nihil est, nisi te scire hoc sciat alter?'
    At pulchrum est digito monstrari et dicier hic est!
ten cirratorum centum dictata fuisse            35
pro nihilo pendas?

      'Ecce inter pocula quaerunt
Romulidae saturi, quid dia poemata narrent.
hic aliquis, cui circa umeros hyacinthia laena est,
rancidulum quiddam balba de nare locutus,             40
Phyllidas Hypsipylas, vatum et plorabile si quid,
eliquat ac tenero supplantat verba palato.
adsensere viri: nunc non cinis ille poetae
felix? non levior cippus nunc inprimit ossa?
laudant convivae: nunc non e manibus illis,            45
nunc non e tumulo fortunataque favilla
nascentur violae?'
              Rides, ait, et nimis uncis
naribus indulges. an erit qui velle recuset
os populi meruisse et cedro digna locutus.            50
linquere nec scombros metuentia carmina nec tus?

    'Quisquis es, o, modo quem ex adverso dicere feci,
non ego cum scribo, si forte quid aptius exit,
quando hoc rara avis est, si quid tamen aptius exit,
laudari metuam, neque enim mihi cornea fibra est;     55
sed recti finemque extremumque esse recuso
euge tuum et belle. nam belle hoc excute totum:
quid non intus habet? non hic est Ilias Atti
ebria veratro? non si qua elegidia crudi
dictarunt proceres? non quidquid denique lectis      60
scribitur in citreis? calidum scis ponere sumen,
scis comitem horridulum trita donare lacerna,
et 'verum' inquis 'amo: verum mihi dicite de me.'
qui pote? vis dicam? nugaris, cum tibi, calve,
pinguis aqualiculus protenso sesquipede extet.      65
o Iane, a tergo quem nulla ciconia pinsit,
nec manus auriculas imitari mobilis albas,
nec linguae, quantum sitiat canis Apula, tantum!
vos, o patricius sanguis, quos vivere fas est
occipiti caeco, posticae occurrite sannae!         70

    'Quis populi sermo est?' quis enim, nisi carmina molli
nunc demum numero fluere, ut per leve severos
ecfundat iunctura unguis? scit tendere versum
non secus ac si oculo rubricam derigat uno.

sive opus in mores, in luxum, in prandia regum                    75
dicere, res grandis nostro dat Musa poetae.
   'Ecce modo heroas sensus adferre videmus
nugari solitos graece, nec ponere lucum
artifices nec rus saturum laudare, ubi corbes
et focus et porci et fumosa Palilia faeno,                         80
unde Remus, sulcoque terens dentalia, Quinti,
quem trepida ante boves dictatorem induit uxor
et tua aratra domum lictor tulit—euge poeta!
   'Est nunc Brisaei quem venosus liber Atti,
sunt quos Pacuviusque et verrucosa moretur                        85
Antiope, aerumnis cor luctificabile fulta.
hos pueris monitus patres infundere lippos
cum videas, quaerisne, unde haec sartago loquendi
venerit in linguas, unde istuc dedecus, in quo
trossulus exsultat tibi per subsellia levis?                      90
   'Nilne pudet capiti non posse pericula cano
pellere, quin tepidum hoc optes audire decenter?
"Fur es" ait Pedio. Pedius quid? crimina rasis
librat in antithetis: doctas posuisse figuras
laudatur "bellum hoc!" hoc bellum? an, Romule, ceves?             95
men moveat qulppe, et, cantet si naufragus, assem
protulerim? Cantas, cum fracta te in trabe pictum
ex umero portes? verum, nec nocte paratum
plorabit, qui me volet incurvasse querella.'
   Sed numeris decor est et iunctura addita crudis.         100
claudere sic versum didicit Berecyntius Attis
et qui caeruleum dirimebat Nerea delphin
sic costam longo subduximus Appennino.
   'Anna virum! nonne hoc spumosum et cortice pingui,
ut ramale vetus vegrandi subere coctum?                           105
quidnam igitur tenerum et laxa cervice legendum?'
   Torva mimalloneis inplerunt cornua bombis,
et raptum vitulo caput ablatura superbo
Bassaris et lyncem Maenas flexura corymbis
euhion ingeminat, reparabilis adsonat echo.                       110
   'Haec fierent, si testiculi vena ulla paterni
viveret in nobis? summa delumbe saliva

hoc natat in labris, et in udo est, Maenas et Attis,
nec pluteum caedit, nec demorsos sapit unguis.'
    Sed quid opus teneras mordaci radere vero       120
auriculas? vide sis, ne maiorum tibi forte
limina frigescant: sonat hic de nare canina littera.
'Per me equidem sint omnia protinus alba;
nil moror. euge! omnes, omnes bene mirae eritis res.
hoc iuvat? "hic" inquis "veto quisquam faxit oletum."    125
pinge duos anguis: pueri, sacer est locus, extra
meite! discedo. secuit Lucilius urbem,
te Lupe, te Muci, et genuinum fregit in illis.
omne vafer vitium ridenti Flaccus amico
tangit et admissus circum praecordia ludit,      130
callidus excusso populum suspendere naso:
me muttire nefas? nec clam, nec cum scrobe?'
       Nusquam.
    'Hic tamen infodiam. vidi, vidi ipse, libelle:
auricilas asini quis non habet? hoc ego opertum,    135
hoc ridere meum, tam nil, nulla tibi vendo
Iliade. Audaci quicumque adflate Cratino
iratum Eupolidem praegrandi cum sene palles,
aspice et haec, si forte aliquid decoctius audis.
inde vaporata lector mihi ferveat aure:      140
non hic, qui in crepidas Graiorum ludere gestit
sordidus, et lusco qui possit dicere 'lusce,'
sese aliquem credens, Italo quod honore supinus
fregerit eminas Arreti aedilis iniquas;
nec qui abaco numeros et secto in pulvere metas    145
scit risisse vafer, multum gaudere paratus,
si cynico barbam petulans nonaria vellat.
his mane edictum, post prandia Calliroën do.'

# SATURA II

Hunc, Macrine, diem numera meliore lapillo,
qui tibi labentis apponit candidus annos.
funde merum genio. non tu prece poscis emaci,
quae nisi seductis nequeas committere divis;
at bona pars procerum tacita libabit acerra.                               5
haut cuivis promptum est murmurque humilisque susurros
tollere de templis et aperto vivere voto.
'Mens bona, fama fides' haec clare et ut audiat hospes;
illa sibi introrsum et sub lingua murmurat 'o si
ebulliat patruus, praeclarum funus!' et 'o si                              10
sub rastro crepet argenti mihi seria dextro
Hercule! pupillumve utinam, quem proximus heres
inpello, expungam! namque est scabiosus et acri
bile tumet. Nerio iam tertia ducitur uxor.'
haec sancte ut poscas, Tiberino in gurgite mergis                          15
mane caput bis terque et noctem flumine purgas.

Heus age, responde—minimum est quod scire laboro—
de Iove quid sentis? estne ut praeponere cures
hunc— 'Cuinam?' cuinam? vis Staio? an scilicet haeres?
quis potior iudex, puerisve quis aptior orbis?                             20
hoc igitur, quo tu Iovis aurem inpellere temptas,
dic agedum Staio, 'pro Iuppiter! o bone' clamet
'Iuppiter!' at sese non clamet Iuppiter ipse?
ignovisse putas, quia, cum tonat, ocius ilex
sulpure discutitur sacro quam tuque domusque?                             25
an quia non fibris ovium Ergennaque iubente
triste iaces lucis evitandumque bidental,
idcirco stolidam praebet tibi vellere barbam
Iuppiter? aut quidnam est, qua tu mercede deorum
emeris auriculas? pulmone et lactibus unctis?                             30

Ecce avia aut metuens divum matertera cunis
exemit puerum frontemque atque uda labella
infami digito et lustralibus ante salivis
expiat, urentis oculos inhibere perita;

tunc manibus quatit et spem macram supplice voto       35
nunc Licini in campos, nunc Crassi mittit in aedis.
'hunc optet generum rex et regina! puellae
hunc rapiant! quidquid calcaverit hic, rosa fiat!'
ast ego nutrici non mando vota: negato,
Iuppiter, haec illi, quamvis te albata rogarit.       40

Poscis opem nervis corpusque fidele senectae.
esto; age; sed grandes patinae tuccetaque crassa
adnuere his superos vetuere Iovemque morantur.

Rem struere exoptas caeso bove Mercuriumque
arcessis fibra. 'Da fortunare Penatis,       45
da pecus et gregibus fetum!' quo, pessime, pacto,
tot tibi cum in flammas iunicum omenta liquescant?
et tamen hic extis et opimo vincere ferto
intendit 'iam crescit ager, iam crescit ovile,
iam dabitur, iam iam!' donec deceptus et exspes       50
nequiquam fundo suspiret nummus in imo.
Si tibi creterras argenti incusaque pingui
auro dona feram. sudes et pectore laevo
excutiat guttas laetari praetrepidum cor.
hinc illud subiit, auro sacras quod ovato       55
perducis facies; nam 'fratres inter aënos
somnia pituita qui purgatissima mittunt,
praecipui sunto sitque illis aurea barba.'
aurum vasa Numae Saturniaque inpulit aera
Vestalisque urnas et Tuscum fictile mutat.       60
o curvae in terris animae et caelestium inanis!
quid iuvat hoc, templis nostros inmittere mores
et bona dis ex hac scelerata ducere pulpa?
haec sibi corrupto casiam dissolvit olivo,
haec Calabrum coxit vitiato murice vellus,       65
haec bacam conchae rasisse et stringere venas
ferventis massae crudo de pulvere iussit.
peccat et haec, peccat; vitio tamen utitur; at vos
dicite, pontifices, in sancto quid facit aurum?
nempe hoc quod Veneri donatae a virgine pupae.       70

quin damus id superis, de magna quod dare lance
non possit magni Messallae lippa propago:
conpositum ius fasque animo sanctosque recessus
mentis et incoctum generoso pectus honesto.
haec cedo ut admoveam templis et farre litabo.                    75

# SATURA III

'Nempe haec adsidue? Iam clarum mane fenestras
intrat et angustas extendit lumine rimas:
stertimus indomitum quod despumare Falernum
sufficiat, quinta dum linea tangitur umbra.
en quid agis? siccas insana canicula messes                          5
iam dudum coquit et patula pecus omne sub ulmo est.'
unus ait comitum. 'verumne? itane? ocius adsit
huc aliquis! nemon?' turgescit vitrea bilis:
'findor'—ut Arcadiae pecuaria rudere dicas.

Iam liber et positis bicolor membrana capillis                       10
inque manus chartae nodosaque venit harundo.
tune querimur, crassus calamo quod pendeat umor,
nigra sed infusa vanescat sepia lympha;
dilutas querimur geminet quod fistula guttas.
o miser inque dies ultra miser, hucine rerum                         15
venimus? a, cur non potius teneroque columbo
et similis regum pueris pappare minutum
poscis et iratus mammae lallare recusas?
'An tali studeam calamo?' Cui verba? quid istas
succinis ambages? tibi luditur, ecfluis amens,                       20
contemnere: sonat vitium percussa, maligne
respondet viridi non cocta fidelia limo.
udum et molle lutum es, nunc nunc properandus et acri
fingendus sine fine rota. sed rure paterno
est tibi far modicum, purum et sine labe salinum—                    25
quid metuas?—cultrixque foci secura patella.
hoc satis? an deceat pulmonem rumpere ventis,
stemmate quod Tusco ramum millesime ducis,
censoremve tuum vel quod trabeate salutas?
ad populum phaleras! ego te intus et in cute novi.                   30
non pudet ad morem discincti vivere Nattae?
sed stupet hic vitio et fibris increvit opimum
pingue, caret culpa, nescit quid perdat, et alto
demersus summa rursum non bullit in unda.

*[These lines have been moved into the following section, Punire Tyrannos*

*Magne pater divum, saevos punire tyrannos*
*haud alia ratione velis, cum dira libido*
*moverit ingenium ferventi tincta veneno:*
*virtutem videant intabescantque relicta.*
*anne magis Siculi gemuerunt aera iuvenci,*
*et magis auratis pendens laquearibus ensis*
*purpureas subter cervices terruit, 'imus,*
*imus praecipites' quam si sibi dicat et intus*
*palleat infelix, quod proxima nesciat uxor?]*

Saepe oculos, memini, tangebam parvus olivo,                    35
grandia si nollem morituri verba Catonis
discere, non sano multum laudanda magistro,
quae pater adductis sudans audiret amicis.
iure: etenim id summum, quid dexter senio ferret,
scire erat in voto; damnosa canicula quantum          40
raderet; angustae collo non fallier orcae ;
neu quis callidior buxum torquere flagello.
haud tibi inexpertum curvos deprendere mores,
quaeque docet sapiens bracatis inlita Medis
porticus, insomnis quibus et detonsa iuventus          45
invigilat, siliquis et grandi pasta polenta:
et tibi quae Samios diduxit littera ramos,
surgentem dextro monstravit limite callem.
stertis adhuc, laxumque caput conpage soluta
oscitat hesternum, dissutis undique malis?          50
est aliquid quo tendis, et in quod derigis arcum?
an passim sequeris corvos testaque lutoque,
securus quo pes ferat, atque ex tempore vivis?

Helleborum frustra, cum iam cutis aegra tumebit,
poscentis videas: venienti occurrite morbo,          55
et quid opus Cratero magnos promittere montis?
discite, o miseri, et causas cognoscite rerum:
quid sumus, et quidnam victuri gignimur; ordo
quis datus, aut metae qua mollis flexus et unde;
quis modus argento, quid fas optare, quid asper          60

utile nummus habet, patriae carisque propinquis
quantum elargiri deceat, quem te deus esse
iussit, et humana qua parte locatus es in re.
disce, nec invideas, quod multa fidelia putet
in locuplete penu, defensis pinguibus Umbris,           65
et piper et pernae, Marsi monumenta clientis,
menaque quod prima nondum defecerit orca.

Hic aliquis de gente hircosa centurionum
dicat 'Quod satis est sapio mihi. non ego curo
esse quod Arcesilas aerumnosique Solones,           70
obstipo capite et figentes lumine terram,
murmura cum secum et rabiosa silentia rodunt
atque exporrecto trutinantur verba labello,
aegroti veteris meditantes somnia, *gigni*
*de nihilo nihilum, in nihilum nil posse reverti.*           75
hoc est, quod palles? cur quis non prandeat, hoc est?'
His populus ridet, multumque torosa iuventus
ingeminat tremulos naso crispante cachinnos.

'Inspice; nescio quid trepidat mihi pectus et aegris
faucibus exsuperat gravis alitus; inspice, sodes!'           80
qui dicit medico, iussus requiescere, posquam
tertia conpositas vidit nox currere venas,
de maiore domo modice sitiente lagoena
lenia loturo sibi Surrentina rogavit.
'Heus, bone, tu palles!' 'Nihil est.' 'Videas tamen istuc,     85
quidquid id est: surgit tacite tibi lutea pellis.'
'At tu detenus palles; ne sis mihi tutor;
iam pridem hunc sepeli: tu restas.' 'Perge, tacebo.'
turgidus hic epulis atque albo ventre lavatur,
gutture sulpureas lente exalante mefites;           90
sed tremor inter vina subit calidumque trientem
excutit e manibus, dentes crepuere retecti,
uncta cadunt laxis tunc pulmentaria labris.
hinc tuba, candelae, tandemque beatulus alto
conpositus lecto crassisque lutatus amomis           95
in portam rigidas calces extendit: at illum

hesterni capite induto subiere Quirites.

'Tange, miser, venas et pone in pectore dextram,
nil calet hic; summosque pedes attinge manusque,
non frigent.' Visa est si forte pecunia, sive                          100
candida vicini subrisit molle puella,
cor tibi rite salit? positum est algente catino
durum holus et populi cribro decussa farina:
temptemus fauces: tenero latet ulcus in ore
putre, quod haud deceat plebeia radere beta.                           105
alges, cum excussit membris timor albus aristas;
nunc face supposita fervescit sanguis et ira
scintillant oculi, dicisque facisque, quod ipse
non sani esse hominis non sanus iuret Orestes.

# PUNIRE TYRANNOS[53]

Magne pater divum, saevos punire tyrannos
haud alia ratione velis, cum dira libido
moverit ingenium ferventi tincta veneno:
virtutem videant intabescantque relicta.
anne magis Siculi gemuerunt aera iuvenci,                    5
et magis auratis pendens laquearibus ensis
purpureas subter cervices terruit, 'imus,
imus praecipites' quam si sibi dicat et intus
palleat infelix, quod proxima nesciat uxor?

---

[53] Tucked away next to verses (with which it is only loosely connected, if at all) in *Satire III*, between lines 34 and 35, *supra*, probably to lessen the risk of an affront to the Emperor.

# SATURA IV

"Rem populi tractas?" barbatnm haec crede magistrum
dicere, sorbitio tollit quem dira cicutae
"quo fretus? dic hoc, magni pupille Pericli.
scilicet ingenium et rerum prudentia velox
ante pilos venit, dicenda tacendaque calles.         5
ergo ubi commota fervet plebecula bile,
fert animus calidae fecisse silentia turbae
maiestate manus. quid deinde loquere? 'Quirites,
hoc puta non iustum est, illud male, rectius illud.'
scis etenim iustum gemina suspendere lance       10
ancipitis librae, rectum discernis, ubi inter
curva subit, vel cum fallit pede regula varo,
et potis es nigrum vitio praefigere theta.
quin tu igitur, summa nequiquam pelle decorus,
ante diem blando caudam iactare popello        15
desinis, Anticyras melior sorbere meracas!
quae tibi summa boni est? uncta vixisse patella
semper et adsiduo curata cuticula sole?
expecta, haud aliud respondeat haec anus, i nunc
'Dinomaches ego sum,' sufla 'sum candidus.' esto;   20
dum ne deterius sapiat pannucia Baucis,
cum bene discincto cantaverit ocima vernae."

Ut nemo in sese temptat descendere, nemo,
sed praecedenti spectatur mantica tergo!
quaesieris 'Nostin Vettidi praedia?' 'Cuius?'     25
'Dives arat Curibus quantum non miluus errat.'
'Hunc ais, hunc dis iratis genioque sinistro,
qui, quandoque iugum pertusa ad compita figit,
seriolae veterem metuens deradere limum
ingemit: *hoc bene sit!* tunicatum cum sale mordens   30
caepe et farratam pueris plaudentibus ollam
pannosam faecem morientis sorbet aceti?'
ac si unctus cesses et figas in cute solem,
est prope te ignotus, cubito qui tangat et acre
despuat 'hi mores! penemque arcanaque lumbi    35

runcantem populo marcentis pandere vulvas!
tu cum maxillis balanatum gausape pectas,
inguinibus quare detonsus gurgulio extat?
quinque palaestritae licet haec plantaria vellant
elixasque nates labefactent forcipe adunca,       40
non tamen ista filix ullo mansuescit aratro.'

"Caedimus, inque vicem praebemus crura sagittis.
vivitur hoc pacto; sic novimus. ilia subter
caecum vulnus habes; sed lato balteus auro
protegit. ut mavis, da verba et decipe nervos,       45
si potes. 'Egregium cum me vicinia dicat,
non credam?' Viso si palles, inprobe, nummo,
si facis in penem quidquid tibi venit amorum:
si puteal multa cautus yibice flagellas:
nequiquam populo bibulas donaveris aures.       50
respue, quod non es; tollat sua munera Cerdo;
tecum habita; noris, quam sit tibi curta supellex."

# SATURA V

'Vatibus hic mos est, centum sibi poscere voces,
centum ora et linguas optare in carmina centum,
fabula seu maesto ponatur hianda tragoedo,
vulnera seu Parthi ducentis ab inguine ferrum.'
'Quorsum haec? aut quantas robusti carminis offas                    5
ingeris, ut par sit centeno gutture niti?
grande locuturi nebulas Helicone legunto,
si quibus aut Prognes, aut si quibus olla Thyestae
fervebit, saepe insulso cenanda Glyconi;
tu neque anhelanti, coquitur dum massa camino,                      10
folle premis ventos, nec clauso murmure raucus
nescio quid tecum grave cornicaris inepte,
nec stloppo tumidas intendis rumpere buccas,
verba togae sequeris iunctura callidus acri,
ore teres modico, pallentis radere mores                           15
doctus et ingenuo culpam defigere ludo.
hinc trahe quae dicis, mensasque relinque Mycenis
cum capite et pedibus, plebeiaque prandia noris.'

'Non equidem hoc studeo, bullatis ut mihi nugis
pagina turgescat, dare pondus idonea fumo.                         20
secreti loquimur; tibi nunc hortante Camena
excutienda damus praecordia, quantaque nostrae
pars tua sit, Cornute, animae, tibi dulcis, amice,
ostendisse iuvat: pulsa, dinoscere cautus,
quid solidum crepet et pictae tectoria linguae.                    25
hic ego centenas ausim deposcere voces,
ut, quantum mihi te sinuoso in pectore fixi,
voce traham pura, totumque hoc verba resignent,
quod latet arcana non enarrabile fibra.

Cum primum pavido custos mihi purpura cessit                       30
bullaque succinctis Laribus donata pependit;
cum blandi comites, totaque inpune Subura
permisit sparsisse oculos iam candidus umbo;
cumque iter ambiguum est et vitae nescius error

deducit trepidas ramosa in compita mentes,                          35
me tibi supposui: teneros tu suscipis annos
Socratico, Cornute, sinu; tum fallere sollers
adposita intortos extendit regula mores,
et premitur ratione animus vincique laborat,
artificemque tuo ducit sub pollice vultum.                          40
tecum etenim longos memini consumere soles,
et tecum primas epulis decerpere noctes:
unum opus et requiem pariter disponimus ambo,
atque verecunda laxamus seria mensa.
non equidem hoc dubites, amborum foedere certo                      45
consentire dies et ab uno sidere duci.
nostra vel aequali suspendit tempora Libra
Parca tenax veri, seu nata fidelibus hora
dividit in Geminos concordia fata duorum,
Saturnumque gravem nostro Iove frangimus una:                      50
nescio quod, certe est, quod me tibi temperat astrum.

Mille hominum species et rerum discolor usus;
velle suum cuique est, nec voto vivitur uno.
mercibus hic Italis mutat sub sole recenti
rugosum piper et pallentis grana cumini,                           55
hic satur inriguo mavult turgescere somno,
hic campo indulget, hunc alea decoquit, ille
in Venerem putris; set cum lapidosa cheragra
fregerit articulos, veteris ramalia fagi,
tunc crassos transisse dies lucemque palustrem                     60
et sibi iam seri vitam ingemuere relictam.

'At te nocturnis iuvat inpallescere chartis;
cultor enim iuvenum purgatas inseris aures
fruge Cleanthea. petite hinc puerique senesque
finem animo certum miserisque viatica canis!'                      65
'Cras hoc fiet.' 'Idem eras fiet.' 'Quid? quasi magnum
nempe diem donas?' Sed cum lux altera venit,
iam cras hesternum consumpsimus: ecce aliud cras
egerit hos annos et semper paulum erit ultra.
nam quamvis prope te, quamvis temone sub uno                       70

vertentem sese, frustra sectabere cantum,
cum rota posterior curras et in axe secundo.

'Libertate opus est: non hac, ut quisque Velina
Publius emeruit, scabiosum tesserula far
possidet. heu steriles veri, quibus una Quiritem                    75
vertigo facit! hic Dama est non tresis agaso,
vappa lippus, et in tenui farragine mendax:
verterit hunc dominus, momento turbinis exit
Marcus Dama. papae! Marco spondente recusas
credere tu nummos? Marco sub iudice palles?                         80
Marcus dixit: ita est; adsigna, Marce, tabellas.
haec mera libertas! hoc nobis pillea donant!
'An quisquam est alius liber, nisi ducere vitam
cui licet, ut voluit? Licet ut volo vivere: non sum
liberior Bruto?' 'Mendose colligis,' inquit                        85
stoicus hic aurem mordaci lotus aceto.
'haec reliqua accipio; *licet* illud et *ut volo* tolle.'
'Vindicta postquam meus a praetore recessi,
cur mihi non liceat, iussit quodcumque voluntas,
excepto si quid Masuri rubrica vetavit?'                           90

'Disce, sed ira cadat naso rugosaque sanna,
dum veteres avias tibi de pulmone revello.
non praetoris erat stultis dare tenuia rerum
officia atque usum rapidae permittere vitae:
sambucam citius caloni aptaveris alto,                             95
stat contra ratio et secretam garrit in aurem,
ne liceat facere id quod quis vitiabit agendo.
publica lex hominum naturaque continet hoc fas,
ut teneat vetitos inscitia debilis actus.
diluis helleborum, certo conpescere puncto                        100
nescius examen? vetat hoc natura medendi.
navem si poscat sibi peronatus arator,
luciferi rudis, exclamet Melicerta perisse
frontem de rebus. tibi recto vivere talo
ars dedit, et veri specimen dinoscere calles,                     105
ne qua subaerato mendosum tinniat auro?

quaeque sequenda forent, quaeque evitanda vicissim,
illa prius creta, mox haec carbone notasti?
es modicus voti? presso lare? dulcis amicis?
iam nunc astringas, iam nunc granaria laxes,                          110
inque luto fixum possis transcendere nummum,
nec glutto sorbere salivam Mercurialem?
"haec mea sunt, teneo" cum vere dixeris, esto
liberque ac sapiens praetoribus ac love dextro;
sin tu, cum fueris nostrae paulo ante farinae,                        115
pelliculam veterem retines, et fronte politus
astutam vapido servas in pectore vulpem,
quae dederam supra relego, funemque reduce.
nil tibi concessit ratio; digitum exere, peccas,
et quid tam parvum est? sed nullo ture litabis,                       120
haereat in stultis brevis ut semuncia recti.
haec miscere nefas; nec, cum sis cetera fossor,
tris tantum ad numeros satyrum moveare Bathylli.'
'Liber ego.' 'Unde datum hoc sentis, tot subdite rebus?
an dominum ignoras, nisi quem vindicta relaxat?'                     125
'I puer et strigiles Crispini ad balnea defer!'
si increpuit, 'cessas nugator?' servitium acre
te nihil inpellit, nec quicquam extrinsecus intrat,
quod nervos agitet; sed si intus et in iecore aegro
nascuntur domini, qui tu inpunitior exis                             130
atque hic, quem ad strigiles scutica et metus egit erilis?

Mane piger stertis. 'Surge!' inquit Avaritia 'heia
surge!' Negas; instat 'Surge!' inquit. 'Non queo.' 'Surge!'
'Et quid agam ?' ' Rogitas? en saperdam advehe Ponto,
castoreum, stuppas, hebenum, tus, lubrica Coa;                       135
tolle recens primus piper ec sitiente camello;
verte aliquid; iura.' 'Sed Iuppiter audiet.' 'Eheu!
baro, regustatum digito terebrare salinum
contentus perages, si vivere cum Iove tendis!'
iam pueris pellem succinctus et oenophorum aptas:                    140
'Ocius ad navem!' nihil obstat, quin trabe vasta
Aegaeum rapias, ni sollers Luxuria ante
seductum moneat 'Quo deinde, insane, ruis? quo?

quid tibi vis? calido sub pectore mascula bilis
intumuit, quod non extinxerit urna cicutae.                          145
tu mare transilias? tibi torta cannabe fulto
cena sit in transtro, Veientanumque rubellum
exalet vapida laesum pice sessilis obba?
quid petis? ut nummos, quos hic quincunce modesto
nutrieras, pergant avidos sudare deunces?                            150
indulge genio, carpamus dulcia! nostrum est
quod vivis; cinis et manes et fabula fies.
vive memor leti! fugit hora; hoc quod loquor inde est.'
en quid agis? duplici in diversum scinderis hamo.
huncine, an hunc sequeris? subeas alternus oportet                   155
ancipiti obsequio dominos, alternus oberres.
nec tu, cum obstiteris semel instantique negaris
parere imperio, 'rupi iam vincula' dicas;
nam et luctata canis nodum abripit; et tamen illi,
cum fugit, a collo trahitur pars longa catenae.                      160

'Dave, cito, hoc credas iubeo, finire dolores
praeteritos meditor:' crudum Chaerestratus unguem
abrodens ait haec. 'An siccis dedecus obstem
cognatis? an rem patriam rumore sinistro
limen ad obscenum frangam, dum Chrysidis udas                        165
ebrius ante fores exstincta cum face canto?'
'Euge, puer, sapias, dis depellentibus agnam
percute.' 'Sed censen plorabit, Dave, relicta?'

'Nugaris; solea, puer, obiurgabere rubra.
ne trepidare velis atque artos rodere casses!                        170
nunc ferus et violens; at si vocet, haud mora, dicas,
*Quidnam igitur faciam? nec nunc, cum accersor et ultro*
*supplicet, accedam? Si totus et integer illinc*
exieras, ne nunc.' hic hic, quod quaerimus, hic est,
non in festuca, lictor quam iactat ineptus.                          175

'Ius habet ille sui palpo, quem ducit hiantem
cretata Ambitio? vigila, et cicer ingere large
rixanti populo, nostra ut Floralia possint
aprici meminisse senes. quid pulchrius? at cum

57

Herodis venere dies, unctaque fenestra                                    180
dispositae pinguem nebulam vomuere lucernae
portantes violas, rubrumque amplexa catinum
cauda natat thynni, tumet alba fidelia vino:
labra moves tacitus recutitaque sabbata palles
tum nigri lemures ovoque pericula rupto,                                  185
tum grandes galli et cum sistro lusca sacerdos
incussere deos inflantis corpora, si non
praedictum ter mane caput gustaveris alii.'

Dixeris haec inter varicosos centuriones,
continuo crassum ridet Pulfennius ingens,                                 190
et centum Graecos curto centusse licetur.

# SATURA VI

Admovit iam bruma foco te, Basse, Sabino?
iamne lyra et tetrico vivunt tibi pectine chordae?
mire opifex numeris veterum primordia vocum
atque marem strepitum fidis intendisse Latinae,
mox iuvenes agitare iocos et pollice honesto                    5
egregius lusisse senex. mihi nunc Ligus ora
intepet hibernatque meum mare, qua latus ingens
dant scopuli et multa litus se valle receptat.
'Lunai portum, est operae, cognoscite, cives!'
cor iubet hoc Enni, postquam destertuit esse                    10
Maeonides Quintus pavone ex Pythagoreo.

Hic ego securus vulgi et quid praeparet auster
infelix pecori, securus et angulus ille
vicini nostro quia pinguior, etsi adeo omnes
ditescant orti peioribus, usque recusem                         15
curvus ob id minui senio aut cenare sine uncto,
et signum in vapida naso tetigisse lagoena.
discrepet his alius! geminos, horoscope, varo
producis genio. solis natalibus est qui
tinguat holus siccum muria vafer in calice empta,              20
ipse sacrum inrorans patinae piper; hic bona dente
grandia magnanimus peragit puer. utar ego, utar,
nec rhombos ideo libertis ponere lautus,
nec tenuis sollers turdarum nosse salivas.

Messe tenus propria vive et granaria, fas est,                  25
emole; quid metuis? occa, et seges altera in herba est.
'Ast vocat officium: trabe rupta Bruttia saxa
prendit amicus inops, remque omnem surdaque vota
condidit Ionio; iacet ipse in litore et una
ingentes de puppe dei, iamque obvia mergis                      30
costa ratis lacerae.' nunc et de caespite vivo
frange aliquid, largire inopi, ne pictus oberret
caerulea in tabula. sed cenam funeris heres
negleget, iratus quod rem curtaveris; urnae

ossa inodora dabit, seu spirent cinnama surdum,          35
seu ceraso peccent casiae, nescire paratus.
tune bona incolumis minuas? et Bestius urguet
doctores Graios, 'Ita fit, postquam sapere urbi
cum pipere et palmis venit nostrum hoc maris expers;
fenisecae crasso vitiarunt unguine pultes.'          40
haec cinere ulterior metuas? At tu, meus heres
quisquis eris, paulum a turba seductior audi.
o bone, num ignoras? missa est a Caesare laurus
insignem ob cladem Germanae pubis, et aris
frigidus excutitur cinis, ac iam postibus arma,          45
iam chlamydes regum, iam lutea gausapa captis
essedaque ingentesque locat Caesonia Rhenos.
dis igitur genioque ducis centum paria ob res
egregie gestas induco; quis vetat? aude.
vae, nisi conives! oleum artocreasque popello          50
largior; an prohibes? die clare! 'Non adeo,' inquis?
exossatus ager iuxta est. Age, si mihi nulla
iam reliqua ex amitis, patruelis nulla, proneptis
nulla manet patrui, sterilis matertera vixit,

deque avia nihilum superest, accedo Bovillas          55
clivumque ad Virbi, praesto est mihi Manius heres.
'Progenies terrae?' Quaere ex me, quis mihi quartus
sit pater: haut prompte, dicam tamen; adde etiam unum,
unum etiam: terrae est iam filius, et mihi ritu
Manius hic generis prope maior. avunculus exit.          60

Qui prior es, cur me in decursu lampada poscis?
sum tibi Mercurius; venio deus huc ego ut ille
pingitur; an renuis? vin tu gaudere relictis?
dest aliquid summae. Minui mihi; sed tibi totum est,
quidquid id est. ubi sit, fuge quaerere, quod mihi quondam    65
legarat Tadius, neu dicta repone paterna.
'fenoris accedat merces; hinc exime sumptus,
quid reliquum est?' Reliquum? nunc, nunc inpensius ungue,
ungue, puer, caules! mihi festa luce coquetur
urtica et fissa fumosum sinciput aure,          70

ut tuus iste nepos olim satur anseris extis,
cum morosa vago singultiet inguine vena,
patriciae inmeiat vulvae? mihi trama figurae
sit reliqua, ast illi tremat omento popa venter?

Vende animam lucro, mercare atque excute sollers          75
omne latus mundi, nec sit praestantior alter
Cappadocas rigida pinguis plausisse catasta:
rem duplica. 'Feci; iam triplex, iam mihi quarto,
iam deciens redit in rugam: depunge, ubi sistam.'
Inventus, Chrysippe, tui finitor acervi.                  80

Latin text from The Satires of A. Persius Flaccus
with a translation and commentary by John Conington, M.A.
Clarendon Press, Oxford, 1893

The text face of the English translation is Adobe Garamond Pro.
The text face of the Latin original is Gill Sans.
The title face is Trajan Pro.

www.ingramcontent.com/pod-product-compliance
Lightning Source LLC
LaVergne TN
LVHW021118080426
835509LV00021B/3441